BILL CASKEY

12 BOLD MOVES

SALES SECRETS TO REINVENT
YOUR SELF AND YOUR RESULTS

Copyright © 2024 by Bill Caskey

All rights reserved. No part of this publication may be reproduced, stored or transmitted in any form or by any means, electronic, mechanical, photocopying, recording, scanning, or otherwise without written permission from the publisher. It is illegal to copy this book, post it to a website, or distribute it by any other means without permission.

Bill Caskey has no responsibility for the persistence or accuracy of URLs for external or third-party Internet Websites referred to in this publication and does not guarantee that any content on such Websites is, or will remain, accurate or appropriate.

If you would like to interview Bill Caskey on your podcast, please reach out to Bill at bcaskey@caskeytraining.com.

To purchase books in large quantities (>25), send request to info@caskeytraining.com.

First edition

TABLE OF CONTENTS

Intro 1

Chapter 1: Create A Sales Process That Benefits The Prospect - (Not Just You) 4

Chapter 2: Start From A Position of "I Don't Know" 13

Chapter 3: Forget About Confidence – Focus On Clarity.... 17

Chapter 4: List The 5 Problems You Solve + ... 23

Chapter 5: Learn How To Say "No" – Respectfully.............. 29

Chapter 6: Interview 5 Clients & Promote Their Success..... 35

Chapter 7: Write Down Your "Intent" & Communicate It ... 42

Chapter 8: Optimize Your Leverage Points.......................... 45

Chapter 9: Get A Coach 51

Chapter 10: Create a Mini Book... 57

Chapter 11: Record an Introductory Video 62

Chapter 12: Declare Your 'Next Step' Offer 66

Additional Training 69

INTRO

I'm delighted that you decided to get this book. I think it's going to change your sales life — maybe forever.

The bottom line is that this content is the best I could find from ALL of our corporate development programs.

All of those communities are like-minded sellers, owners, and creators who, at the very least, want to grow their business and their income.

I went back and transcribed all of those meetings and assembled what I think are the 12 best business moves to make as you seek to grow.

I'll be honest with you - there were a whole lot more than 12 that I found. I had 50 that I had documented and it was a monumental struggle to get it down to 12. But I believe these 12 are THE most important.

Each concept is followed with why it is important to you. Then, I include some ideas on implementation so you can deploy this in your business.

If you're like me and don't like to wade through 300-page books JUST to get the 12 nuggets - I've saved you time by just giving you the nuggets.

Enjoy.

What is Bold?

"Boldness has genius, power, and magic in it." -Goethe

Boldness takes courage. Though the following 12 moves may seem like common sense, few actually put them into practice. I define boldness as: Possessing the confidence to pursue desires without fear to make daring choices that defy the status quo.

While some suggestions may not seem audacious, they remain uncommon in action. Don't let that deter you.

My aim is to embolden you to deploy new strategies to equip you with the adventurous spirit required for meaningful change, regardless of any existing orthodoxy holding you back.

Progress demands bravery. These pages call on you to be bold, to tap into your inner genius, power, and magic—the innate ingredients of boldness itself.

You may read a suggestion and think, "That's not bold; that's just common sense." And you're right. They are common sense. But common sense is not common practice. Therein lies the distinction.

I have curated 12 bold moves seldom acted upon. Do not allow perceived simplicity to preclude implementation. Use this book to find the courage to follow your heart and take the risks necessary to live your dreams.

Boldness means different things to different people. For some, a concept deemed simple may require great daring. If these strategies resonate yet remain unutilized, then boldly put them into action.

Allow fresh thinking to awaken your inner boldness.

Progress takes audacity. Be adventurous. Be brave. Be bold.

CHAPTER 1

CREATE A SALES PROCESS THAT BENEFITS THE PROSPECT - (NOT JUST YOU)

People are happy to follow your process if they knew what it was. So tell them.

I've been coaching for the last 30 years, primarily in the business-to-business space. And I've worked with hundreds of companies – thousands of individuals.

And it always baffles me how few companies have a sales process that their people adhere to. I guess salespeople are just not 'process' people. We prefer to wing it, and use our gift of gab and our **vibe** to attract clients. Bad idea.

The problem with that thinking is the customer needs to know **where you're taking them.** And if they don't, it's unlikely they'll follow you.

So I want you to create a sales process that benefits them, whether they buy or not.

Why It's Good For You

- It helps you know where you are at all times during the sales process. It keeps you on track.
- It helps you articulate the journey for your prospect. This is especially valuable in longer selling Cycles.
- It helps you troubleshoot where prospects fall off the journey. For VPS of sales and sales managers, this is an invaluable tool to help you improve the skills of your team in certain areas of the process where they're weaker.

Why It's Good For Your Prospects

- People intrinsically want to know where you're taking them and what the journey looks like. If they do, they'll be more likely to follow it.
- Prospects want to feel like they're in good hands with you. they want to have confidence that you know what you're doing. A good process turns you into a pro overnight.

Step 1. The Sales Process

The sales process should be a **map** of the sale, both for you and your prospect. It should be something you share with them – something that is visual. If it's not documented, it's not followed.

And if it's not visual, it's hard to share with a prospect.

What are the components of a good sales process?

We could write a whole book about that, but here are several I think are important.

1-Some type of upfront understanding or discovery mechanism.

It could be a call, a survey, an audit, or a face-to-face meeting. But at the beginning, you want to set the table with your prospect of, "Here's who I am. Here's how I might be able to help. Here are the kinds of problems we solve. And here is the roadmap to help us find out together if we're a fit or not. And as we go through this, we can decide together if we even want to have a second call."

That first discovery call is a **mutual understanding meeting.** We're just trying to figure each other out to see if there's anything here.

2-The second call is more in-depth.

Maybe it includes some of their people and some of your people, or maybe it's just you and them. But if you're in a larger ticket (+$10K)/ or complex sale (60-120 days), a second meeting is appropriate to get other perspectives.

If other people are involved in the decision or influencing the decision to buy or not buy from you, then **they need to be a part of some process.**

3- The next step is an analysis.

It might be done by you or somebody inside your company. But there is a good reason to have a step where you analyze what you've learned in the "discovery" phase and then come back to them with a recommendation.

An example

We have a client who's in the medical records business. there are tons of people in that business, and they call on the same people over and over again. Talk to a manager of a clinic and ask them how many calls you get each day from medical records people, and you'll be astonished at the number.

We coached our client to tell the prospect up front:

"We don't know if we can help you solve a problem mainly because we don't even know what the problem is or if there is one. So we've developed a **Rapid Financial Assessment** *where we take some of the data you're comfortable sharing–and then analyze it so we can tell you if we can help. Once you see the analysis, you will be able to tell whether we can bring economic value to you."*

You see, the key element there is that "We don't know if we can help, but this analysis will give both of us a peek inside your business to determine if we can bring value."

When you have a good process, you can enter the dialog from an "I don't know" position.

That's important because that position will help create the environment where they are comfortable sharing data.

4- A recommendation of some kind.

You are a) recapping the problem that they said they had and b) expressing the impact of that problem on them or their business. You are sharing your findings based on the questioning/surveying that you have done. Then, you recommend a course of action.

I like calling this a **Recommendation** phase rather than a **Presentation** phase. I don't want to associate myself with the amateur salesperson who's always in **'present'** mode. You're better than that.

Think of yourself as a surgeon, where you are doing the lab work and the research, and then you're **recommending** to the patient what the options are.

About Too Many Options

One thing about options: Be careful about providing too many. **I like two options.** The confused mind never buys, and I don't confuse the buyer with too many different recommendations.

If you just have one recommendation, that's great. I like two because I think it gives people a chance to either buy in quickly or upsell themselves.

We have a client in the software business who always offers two options:

Option 1 is a fast-track option that helps them get their problem solved quickly. It's obviously more expensive.

And Option 2 is a longer-term solution.

It depends on the nature of the company's implementation history as to which one they select. That's why we like two solutions.

Their Results

We have found that 30% of their prospects select the **fast track** option (1) and 70% the longer term option. They have increased their business by 25% because of the fact that the fast-track option is a higher ticket option.

4-Tweaking

There's bound to be something that comes up that's in the way of the sale, and you will need to navigate that. Leave space here for doing that. It should be part of your process. If there is no tweaking to be done, leave it out. But most of the time, in large sales, there is modification that must happen.

We like to put this in the process so that we aren't going back and forth at the end trying to figure out what the next steps are. If you put it in upfront and allow them to see that it's just a natural part of our system, they are more likely to follow it.

Step 2. Something In It For Them

Is the sales process itself beneficial for them? I would say it is, especially if you're not pitching and presenting the whole time – but asking them questions that get to the heart of the matter.

The fact is that when you are selling to someone who is not quite sure if your solution is perfect for them, you must prove that you know what you're doing. I believe the best way to do that is to be **rigorous with your assessment.** I want you to have confidence in yourself, but I also want them to have confidence in you.

And there's no better way to do that than to be **obsessed** with their circumstances and pains. The process will help you do that.

I think you also should have something **in it for them,** like a "**Findings & Recommendation**" document or some type of in-depth analysis that you deliver.

That way, you can say to the prospect, "We will provide you an in-depth findings and recommendation document. And whether you engage with us or not, this will be helpful for you if you choose to find another vendor - or try fixing it yourself."

You might not say it in those exact words, but if you create a **findings** document and they say, "I'm going to go somewhere else," you can't stop them. The **Bold Move** here is that you are detached and of massive help to them without strings attached.

Plus, you create more **detachment and more abundant thinking** when you offer something that they can use elsewhere.

A Note on Detachment

If you've followed my podcast, The Bill Caskey Podcast, for any length of time, you know how important I believe **Detachment** is throughout the sales process. The more **attached** you are to the result, the more likely you are to get in the way of the selling cycle.

And that's the last thing I want – for you to get in the way. Detachment offers you the freedom to control the sales process without bias.

In the companion audiobook, I go into more detail on Detachment.

The Bottom Line

Something must be a part of the sales process that's of benefit to them, whether they buy from you or not. It will help you become more rigid about them following your process because you **know it will be a benefit to them** with no expectation.

CHAPTER 2

START FROM A POSITION OF "I DON'T KNOW"

There is more you don't know than know. So why not turn that into a strategic advantage?

This concept blows away traditional thinkers. But it shouldn't if you think about it the right way.

We've always been taught to be eager, have high expectations, and always be closing. After more than 30 years of training and coaching sales teams, spending over 20,000 hours in training sessions, I've come to the realization that **eagerness is garbage.**

It takes away from your professionalism. You can be eager to help the customer identify the problems without being eager for the sale. That's the ideal scenario.

Therefore, a better way to think about your conduct in the sales cycle is to enter it in the spirit of "I don't know if I can help." Because the fact is **you don't know.** So, A, it's the truth and B, it helps create an atmosphere for trust between you and your prospect.

And shouldn't <u>trust</u> be the core mission of any first engagement or contact with a prospect? The answer is **yes**, it should. But if we revert to selling too quickly, convincing and persuading, all that trust evaporates – if it was there in the first place.

Sadghguru is one of my favorite ancient yogis, and he says you might as well be in a state of "I don't know" because there's a whole lot more you don't know than do know. So, if you want to play with the infinite, play in the sandbox of "I don't know."

Treatment

You can find your own way to voice it, when to use it, and how to use it. Maybe the words aren't exactly what I've given you here, but find your own words that fit your personality and the context of the calls you're making.

A Story Helps

You can even tell a short story when you enter into the process.

You could say something like, "You know, when I first got into sales, I used to assume that I knew everything about the prospect because I had done research and called on many people like you. What I soon found out was I was wrong 90% of the time. So now, I enter these discussions with new prospects from the state of "I don't know" because there's a whole lot more I don't know than I do – and if you don't mind, I'd like to ask you some questions to help me understand whether I can be of value to you."

That is magic because it's the truth. And if you state it the way I did in the paragraph above, the prospect will gain trust in you.

Maintain That Posture

You don't want a surgeon to say, "I don't know if I can help," as he's cutting you open. You have to have confidence in that surgeon. But he **will** say upfront, "I don't know what the best possible solution is until we do some lab work."

For you, I would maintain the "I don't know" position for as long as you can. As long as you maintain that position, the customer is sharing more information with you, which is not a bad thing.

But when you get to the Recommendation phase, now you are certain. You lose the 'I don't know' position and take up the position of "I have done the analysis based on your input, and I believe we can help you."

Try it. Today.

No reason to wait. Try it in your next first meeting. Heck, before you do that, speak it into existence by recording yourself. Play it back. See how it sounds.

If it's not quite where you want it, re-record it. Do it again until it sounds organic.

It must sound genuine because it IS genuine. You don't know more than you know.

CHAPTER 3

FORGET ABOUT CONFIDENCE – FOCUS ON CLARITY

Confidence is the currency we use to take risks - to get out of our comfort zone. Get clear - and confidence ensues.

Confidence is one of those things that we all need more of, but we're afraid to talk about needing it.

Not sure why that is. I guess it's just our ego. We're petrified of saying that we lack confidence in an endeavor.

So, let's **back** into confidence. I don't think you achieve confidence by going off to the Himalayas for 6 months. Your work may slow down if you did that. 🙂

But I do think you gain confidence by becoming **crystal clear** about those things that you have less confidence in than you should.

About 2 years ago, I had the chance to go to the Enchantment Resort in Sedona, Arizona. If you haven't been, it's stunning. it sits at the foot of some amazing rock formations and mountains.

There was a meditation center in the resort where I had a chance to talk to the manager. He was steeped in meditation and mindfulness. I asked him how people got confidence, and he said very quickly, "Confidence is all about clarity."

His answer to how one gets clarity, obviously, was sit in meditation, or stillness. When you do that, clarity ensues. But meditation is not what this chapter is about.

I only give that to you because I find today that a lot of people lack Clarity about where they're going, how they'll get there, what role they play in life, and what their Divine Mission is. So, if you're facing some of those struggles, I would suggest a mindfulness practice of some kind where you can slow down your thinking and allow what's deep to bubble up. That will help for clarity.

Exercise

Privately, in the space below, write down three areas in which you lack confidence. Show it to no one. 🙂

1:

2:

3:

Now, go back to each one of those and ask yourself, "What am I not clear about here?"

Example

One of the things I find people lack confidence in is how and when to bring up **money**.

Every trainer has their own framework of when and how to bring it up. But we're all different, and the best thing we can do is become clear about HOW to bring it up. Then, the WHEN will take care of itself.

If we're afraid of bringing it up, there is never the right WHEN.

Here are some things you might become clearer on about money. (This is just an example – I am not suggesting you have a problem here.)

- Money is simply the exchange of value–they get your solution - and you get their compensation for that solution. It's a respectable exchange.
- If your solution/product isn't VALUABLE to the customer, they won't exchange money for it. So your goal should be to understand the pains and dilemmas that they face, along with the payoff they expect from working with you, and that will improve your value significantly.
- People KNOW they will have to pay money for something they want.
- What they spend is ALWAYS juxtaposed (been looking for a reason to use that word :) to what they get. That's why it's important to denominate the problem they have and their life without a solution. Then, when you talk about your price, it seems like a great deal.
- Pre-warn them where in the process you want to have this conversation. You might say something like, "At some point today or in our next meeting, I want to have an **economics conversation** with you where we understand clearly any price you might pay for not solving the problem versus the price you pay to solve it. That's what we mean by economics."

See how that works? There are six bullets that you probably didn't think of when it came to money.

Each one improves your clarity about how to talk about it. It gives you the confidence to have that conversation whenever it comes up organically.

Another way to create Clarity is to **examine the beliefs** that hold you back. Becoming clear about your limiting beliefs is a form of clarity. It will lead to confidence because you'll examine those beliefs and realize that some are outdated.

A Quick Note on Beliefs

When you think about how you arrived at your beliefs in life, they probably came from your culture, parents, adolescent mentoring, or maybe your first manager.

Unfortunately, you have to constantly take stock of your beliefs to make sure that they are helping you get where you want to go.

One thing I find about high achievers, whom I work with a lot, is they are never reluctant to examine their beliefs. In fact, they often say, "I like what you're saying here, Bill, but how do I change my thinking to allow me to do this behavior?"

If there's something you know you need to do but have procrastinated, it's probably because your beliefs are not congruent with that new behavior. So examine them.

Yes, sometimes it takes another human being there to work through that with you, but you can do a lot of this on your own.

Exercise

Now, do the same exercise for those **three areas of confidence** that you had. Just use a bullet-pointed list. You'll be shocked at how much more confidence will ensue in those areas.

CHAPTER 4

LIST THE 5 PROBLEMS YOU SOLVE +

If you want to earn more, be clearer about the problems you solve. The bigger the problems, the bigger the check.

This chapter solves two problems: 1) how you talk about your value and 2) what you can do to share your value on video platforms.

Why Problems?

Problems are what you are put on this planet to solve. You do it in your personal life, in your sports life, in your church life, and in other areas, too.

Life presents you with a never-ending series of challenges and problems that you work to navigate.

And in sales, we are always talking about value.

But what is value? **Value** is the intersection between a) your solution, b) **the problem someone has that your solution would fix**, and c) the destination they want to get to when they solve that problem.

The List of Problems

By making a list of the problems you solve, you will become more savvy at communicating your value to your prospect. After all, the prospect doesn't give 2 damns about your solution – **until** it can help them solve or avoid a problem—or help them get to a new future.

So, focusing on problems is critical.

Note: When I ask my clients to do this, they typically revert to what they do for people. That is not this. I want you to focus on **their** problems, **their** dilemmas, **their** circumstances they are faced with.

Some of these problems might be problems they know they have. And others they might be blind to. In the space below, I've asked you to do two lists.

Problems They Know They Have

An Example: In my business, when I call on VPS of sales, one of the problems they know they have is that their salespeople are not making enough calls and not uncovering enough opportunities. So that would be my number 1.

1:

2:

3:

4:

5:

Problems They DON'T Know They Have

An Example: Using that same VP example, one of the problems they don't know they have is their salespeople are unclear about the proper way to do cold outreach. They think all their people know how to do that. In my experience, they don't. So I would put this down for number 1

1:

2:

3:

4:

5:

The Video

I believe that your true potential is on the other side of the assets that you leverage. If you want to reach it or scale your income, get better at leveraging your assets. I talk about that in a later chapter.

But video is a key asset you have available.

If you have a phone, you should be shooting more videos to post on social platforms.

But the question is always, "What do I say?"

Now, it's time to take each of those problems and create a short video. Title the video with a question that refers to that problem.

So let's imagine that one of the problems you solve is customers **spending too much on X product, and they're frustrated about this.** So the title of your video would be, "How do I reduce my expenses on x product so I can be more profitable?"

Do you see how that works? **Take the problem and turn it into a question** that they might ask.

Why? Questions meet them where they are. if you get too elaborate with your video title, it requires too much brain power (and calories for them to make the link.) But if you make the title of the video **exactly** what they might be asking themselves, it will be a winner.

Then, shoot a video where you answer that question.

You're not giving them everything. You're giving them a sense that you know what you're talking about – and how you relate to the important problem they have.

The Side Benefit

A side benefit of being problem-focused is that you are always **searching for problems** when you're in conversation with people. And you will be less likely to switch to product-pitch mode if you haven't identified the core problem yet.

A Model

We have a very simple model we use in our coaching practice. It's designed to help you get higher on the triangle. At the bottom of the triangle is product. That's when all you talk about are the features and Technical aspects of your product. while there's nothing wrong with that, that's not where we begin.

The middle section is the **solution**. That's better than talking about the product, but it only takes you so far.

A better place to be on the triangle is the top section, **the transformation.** What transformation do you suspect your prospect will experience if they buy your product, which will give them a solution to their problems and take them to a new place?

I tell my corporate coaching clients and high-income individuals always to be focused on the transformation. If you are tempted to slip back into product or solution mode, be thinking, **"What is the transformation this solution will make in their lives?"**

If you get really good at this, you will be unstoppable. I promise. Few do this.

Remember, the high-income seller solves bigger problems than the low-income seller. And how do you solve them? **You become clear about what they are first.**

Video Record The Top 5 Solutions To Their Problems

"If you want to earn more, be clearer about the problems you solve. The bigger the problems, the bigger the check."

CHAPTER 5

LEARN HOW TO SAY "NO" – RESPECTFULLY

Highly paid professionals are willing to work only on those things where there is a payoff.

First of all, it makes perfect sense to address WHY you should get "no" into your mind and heart. This is not about discounting people - it's about you taking care of your energy.

A Few Reasons Why

1. Preserve Integrity: Saying no to unethical practices, unfair deals, or situations that compromise your values helps maintain your professional integrity and reputation. In our work, we talk about building your personal brand - another way to say that is building your reputation. Integrity is a key part of reputation.

2. It Focuses Your Energy: Saying no to non-essential tasks or commitments allows you to prioritize and dedicate your time and resources to the most important goals and high-impact activities. I don't want you to waste energy chasing bad deals.

3. Avoids Overcommitment: Learning to say no prevents you from taking on more than you can handle, which can lead to missed deadlines, subpar work, and burnout. We all have the tendency to chase shiny objects, and sometimes those objects are in the form of a prospect who is likely never going to be a customer.

4. Builds Boundaries: Saying 'no' establishes healthy boundaries, both professionally and personally, preventing others from taking advantage of your time and efforts. Time is the currency that you trade for your goals and your vision. If there are no boundaries, you will end up sucking time that you could be using for more profitable endeavors.

5. Increases Confidence: The ability to respectfully decline requests or offers demonstrates confidence in your decision-making abilities and self-assurance. We've already talked about confidence at length. This is a huge confidence builder. I want you to say no to prospects who won't follow your process.

6. Enhances Negotiation Power: Saying no can be a powerful negotiation tactic, allowing you to walk away from deals that don't align with your interests or expectations. But remember, "no" is not a sales move. It is not here to get the customer to say "yes." It is here because I want you to be frugal with your time and only pursue deals that are good for everybody

7. Fosters Respect: When you say no firmly but politely, you command respect from colleagues, clients, and business partners, as they recognize your boundaries and priorities.

8. Improves Decision-Making: Saying no gives you the mental space and clarity to make better decisions, rather than being driven by the pressure to say yes to every opportunity.

9. Maintains Work-Life Balance: Knowing when to say no to additional commitments or projects helps you maintain a healthy work-life balance and avoid burnout.

I see this with a lot of sales/leaders--burnout. I want you to be fresh every day - and the way to do that is to say 'no' to lousy opportunities.

10. Encourages Authenticity: By saying no to opportunities or clients that don't align with your values or goals, you can stay true to your authentic self and the vision for your business.

In sales, you are always faced with a decision: **Do I pursue or not?**

You might have a prospect who, on the first call, gives you all the information you need but then cools down as you move through the sales process. At some point, you may need to tell them, "This is not a fit for us."

Or, you may have a buttoned-down process that your customer just doesn't want to follow. And you know that if they don't follow it, the likelihood of you closing the business goes way down.

Therefore, you must find a way to say, "Based on where we are now, I'm not sure it makes any sense to continue."

Lots of Ways To Say It

There are lots of ways to say "No." But you must change your mindset to the belief that **your time is extremely valuable.** And if you're closing 15% of the deals you propose right now, you have a lot of NOs you need to say.

Another way to say it is to bring it up as HERE'S WHY. "I appreciate you asking me to make this concession, but I won't be able to do that, and here's why." It's better if you can give a rationale as to **why** you can't do it so they understand your dilemma.

Be nice though. People don't like being told **no**, so you have to cushion it a little. Keep them OK through this conversation.

Quick Note On OK/Not OK

We have been teaching this psychological principle for over 30 years, and it's as valuable today as it ever was. The fact is that everything you say or do in the buyer/seller dance has the potential to make the prospect OK or not OK.

Things That Make Them Not OK

- Pushing too hard too quickly.
- Convincing them without knowing the background of their problem.
- Asking them questions that come out of nowhere and make them uncomfortable.
- Interrupting them as they're telling you about their issues.
- Disagreeing with something they've said without going deeper on it first.

- Expecting them to follow you without giving them the map.
- Telling them no without giving them a rationale as to why

If you're not used to saying "No," it can be vexing. But the best thing you can do is start - practice. And start in low-risk situations. If you're selling to Boeing, don't start there. :)

"No's" save you tons of time chasing people who will never buy.

CHAPTER 6

INTERVIEW 5 CLIENTS & PROMOTE THEIR SUCCESS

It's a lot easier to get a meeting with someone if your aim is to spotlight their goodness.

This will put you out of your comfort zone. But after all, that's what **"Bold Moves"** is all about – expanding your comfort zone. My suggestion is you take five clients you have worked with for a while and do an interview with them on Zoom, where you spotlight their business. (This works for prospects, too).

Why Are We Suggesting This?

- **Builds Deeper Connections:** Hearing clients' personal stories and struggles helps build a stronger emotional connection and rapport with them. Isn't that what you want?
- **Provides Valuable Insights:** Learning about clients' challenges and how they resolve them can offer insights into their mindset, values, and decision-making processes. Think about the people who will listen to this - bring value to them.
- **Highlights Resilience:** Hearing about clients' ability to overcome adversity showcases their resilience and determination, which can be inspiring and motivating for the audience. Plus, you are bound to hear something about them you did not know. People open up when being interviewed.
- **Generates Empathy:** Learning about clients' journeys fosters empathy and a deeper understanding of their unique circumstances and experiences.

- **Identifies Growth Opportunities:** Clients' stories may reveal areas for improvement or new opportunities for growth within your business. This is not WHY you're doing it - but it is a by-product.
- **Builds Trust and Credibility:** Showing genuine interest in clients' narratives demonstrates care and builds trust, enhancing your credibility as a business.
- **Creates Engaging Content:** Client stories can be powerful marketing tools, providing authentic and relatable content that resonates with potential customers.

Format

I suggest you do the **Story–Setback–Ascension** format.

Ask them about their **Story**...how they grew up...what kinds of situations they faced in their life as they pursued their success.

Then, talk about **Setbacks**. Maybe they didn't get into the college they wanted to get into - or maybe the job they really wanted fell apart - or maybe they realized the path they were going down was not the right path.

Those are all setbacks. It's the key to a great story. The ability to share setbacks so that those in the listening audience can relate.

Then comes the **Ascension** part of the story. How they have ascended from where they were to where they are today. You could ask them about books they've read, coaches they've had, advice they've been given.

Prospects

I have several clients who interview prospects that they want to learn more about. Very few people will say "no" to an interview if your mission is to **Spotlight their goodness.**

Example

We are going to be launching a sales leadership program sometime in the next 12 months. One of my strategies is to interview 12 sales managers/leaders and ask them what some of their issues are, what some of their wins have been, and how they motivate a sales team.

I will probably turn that into some sort of a "pop-up" podcast series. Just 12 interviews is all. But at the end of each interview (off camera), I will share with them some of the work that I'm doing with other sales leaders – and ask if they would like to get some information on how they can be a part of that. Very soft sell.

They get to share their wisdom. I get to know them better. Who loses there? No one.

Make a list of the first five prospects or customers that you can interview and go to it. Use Zoom. Don't overcomplicate this. Somebody in your company can probably help you create a pop-up podcast. The cost of this is less than $100. Spend $100 to earn 50K. I like that return. And you?

And, before you know it, you'll have people calling YOU wanting to be on your show. The advanced version of this is to make it an ongoing show, either on YouTube, LinkedIn, or a simple podcast. **Bold** enough for you? Thought so.

Use

OK, so you finished the interviews, and now it's time to use them. So how do you do that? Here are seven ideas:

1. Create a Client Testimonial Video Series: Edit the interviews into compelling video testimonials and share them on your website, social media channels, and other digital platforms to showcase your satisfied clients' experiences. Take the best parts of the 5 and create clips from them. Put it on your website

www.yourcompany.com/clientstories.

2. Develop a Case Study Library: If you are talking with these clients about your solutions (which likely will come up), then compile the interviews into comprehensive case studies, highlighting each client's unique journey, challenges, and how your solutions helped them succeed. Share these on your website and in sales materials. (If this is purely a 'spotlight' on them - and you aren't bringing up your work with them, then skip this one.)

3. Publish a Blog Series: Turn the interviews into a series of blog posts - or LinkedIn articles, each focusing on a different client's story. In addition to LI, repurpose them and share on your company's blog to provide valuable insights and inspire potential customers.

4. Produce a Podcast: Consider turning the video interviews into a podcast series, allowing your clients to share their stories in their own words and voices, which can be more engaging and personal. You can create a pop-up podcast very easily. Just Google it. (Another nice thing about this is that as you seek to interview more people, you can give people a sample by sending them to your podcast.)

5. Create Social Media Highlights: Extract powerful quotes, statistics, or memorable moments from the interviews and share them as social media posts or graphics to engage your followers and spark interest in your brand. We call this a "clip strategy," taking short clips from your interview and posting them on social media.

6. Develop an Email Marketing Campaign: Incorporate excerpts or highlights from the interviews into your email marketing campaigns. Don't forget to promote these interviews to your email list. Don't promote all five at one time though. I suggest breaking down each interview into five important elements and promoting it with five different emails. Get creative here.

7. Incorporate into Sales Presentations: Integrate relevant client stories and testimonials from the interviews into your sales presentations and proposals to demonstrate the value you've provided to others in similar situations. I simply take the video and pop it into a keynote or PowerPoint presentation slide, and presto, you have a way to bring your client's voice into a presentation.

Again, #7 applies if your client Spotlight includes testifying to your competence.

CHAPTER 7

WRITE DOWN YOUR "INTENT" & COMMUNICATE IT

An underused asset is your "intention." Make your intention about helping others solve big problems.

Write Down Your "Intent" & Communicate It

How many times have you lost a sale or experienced a cool reception to your message? If you've been in sales longer than 30 days, you've probably felt that.

What's happening here? Is what you're saying off? Is the prospect just not the right person? Or is there something deeper? Well, you know me by now...and I say the problem is deeper. I think the problem is **low intent**.

What is Intent?

Intent is that deep-seated feeling about our **why** or our goals in a particular situation. It's your underlying purpose or aim.

If I go to a networking event and my intent is to **sell** five people at that event, people will see me coming and sprint away. Even if they haven't sprinted for 30 years. :)

But if my intent is to go to this event and bring value to people as I speak with them, and if they want to talk further about my product, I'm happy to do that, but I'm not attached to that...don't you think my results change? And don't you think I will attract people to me?

Of course. Think of intent as a "deeper purpose."

The problem we have when we conduct the sales process is **competing intentions**. Your intention is to make the sale. Their intention is to get information and get the product at the lowest price. **Those intentions are at odds.**

So I want you to change your intention. Write out the following, practice it, and deliver it on every first call.

"My intention today is to understand a bit more about your business and we can determine together whether - or IF I can be of value to you. My goal is to be a resource to help you whether we engage or not."

Rule

Always share your intention. If new people enter the sales process, make it clear to them what your intention is. Your actions follow your intention. And the best thing you can do is to get on the same page with your prospect.

When you do this correctly, and it comes from the heart, you'll be surprised at how this simple micro-tool changes the entire dynamic between buyer and seller. I know this might not sound like a **bold** move, but few do it. That's what makes it **bold**.

Again, you want your intentions to align with theirs. And this will do that.

CHAPTER 8

OPTIMIZE YOUR LEVERAGE POINTS

Leverage is the master key to realizing your true potential. We all have assets we fail to use.

I run an online program called The Million Dollar Seller. You can find out more about it here if you're inclined (www.billcaskey.com/milliondollarseller.) The essence of that program is that you **cannot get to exponentially higher levels of income just by doing more behavior.** There's not enough time – it will wear you out.

My second lesson in that program is that sales training will only get you so far. Yes, you can develop better in-person, face-to-face sales skills, but there is a limit on how good you can be in front of people.

The Skill Of Leverage

Call it leverage, or optimization, or maximization. You pick the term, but the idea is that **you have assets that are available to you that you don't use.** Maybe they are relationships you have with customers. Maybe it's technology that you're good at. Maybe it's problem-solving frameworks that you've created.

But most of those aren't leveraged to the fullest. So, my goal in this chapter is to expand your thinking about what your "assets" are and to begin your journey to leveraging them better.

Leverage & Assets

First, let's define both terms: **assets and leverage.**

Assets: A useful or valuable thing, person or quality.

I know this is a rather vague definition, but it's a good start for us. I believe we have assets in areas we don't even think to look.

Here's a quick list:

- The relationships you've developed over the years with other human beings.
- The list of solutions that you've implemented in your client's business.
- Your client stories of how you help them transform their results.
- The email list you have accumulated over the years of acquaintances, prospects, and partners.
- The technology that exists in your phone.
- Your story.
- Your company story.
- Your ability and talent.
- Your ability to speak and tell stories.
- Your knowledge of the industry you're in.

To be honest, the list never ends. But I'll bet you never thought of these things as assets. You might have thought of them as tools, like your phone. I think they're more than that.

Leverage: Use of a thing to it's maximum advantage to get to a desired outcome.

Just think about, "How do I use this asset that I have in a way that would maximize its output?"

Document Your Leverage Points

So the exercise here is for you to document those assets that, if you used them more frequently, you could generate more income in the marketplace. I gave you some samples above.

A simple start is **technology**. This is a perfect place to begin because we all have access to technology. Our phone. Our laptop. The social media platforms that we're on. So rate your use of that technology between zero and 10, where zero is "I'm not using it at all," and 10 is "I'm a **super leverager."**

Technology | 0—1–2–3–4–5–6–7–8–9–10

Now, write down three ways you can leverage technology (that you already have) in your world. I am not suggesting to buy more tech. **Use what you have.** That's the idea of leverage – **using assets that you already possess.**

1:

2:

3:

Example of Eric

Eric is one of my clients in [The Million Dollar Seller](#) program. He identified he is under-utilizing **the questions that prospects ask him** in the sales process.

I'll bet that it didn't occur to you that the questions you get asked are an asset. That's okay. Bear with me.

So, he decided to do a short LinkedIn video every time a prospect asked him a question. And he would provide a short answer.

Think about it. He's already in front of prospects or on the phone with them. He's done the work to get there, And he fields hundreds of questions a year. Yet **he was doing nothing with those questions.**

He found that many of his prospects would see these questions on LinkedIn, and they would have **exactly** the same question. So, they would watch the video and reach out to him for more information.

Bold enough? My suggestion is to do this for 90 days. Shoot 12 videos - one a week. See what happens. If you want to begin now (I love fast action takers :) start with making a list of the questions you typically get at various parts of the funnel.

Top of Funnel Questions - The Best

These are questions that come right as you and the prospect begin talking. Here are five that you could use as videos:

1. Why should I be looking at (xxx)?
2. What are some considerations as I explore solutions around (xxx)?

3. What are some mistakes I might be making in the area of xxx that I'm unaware of?
4. Why should solving this problem matter?
5. What do people overlook when considering solving this problem?

These are right off the top of my head but you would likely have 12 to 20 more questions. Just put yourself in the customer's shoes and think about what questions they would have early in the process.

CHAPTER 9
GET A COACH

Nothing will speed you to higher potential than having a coach shine the light on your blind spots.

Yes, this can be a massive move – and it might cost you money. I purchase a lot of coaching from people each year. I've probably spent $250,000 over the last 10 years hiring people who can look at my business and strategies - and find holes that I'm unaware of.

Investing in yourself **ALWAYS** provides a return, and it's much higher than you get in the stock market.

It's amazing to me how we fret about 8, 9, and 12% returns in the market when investing in **yourself** can yield a **10 to 100x return.** We're majoring in the minors.

The Jimmy Webb Story

Jimmy Webb is a popular country music writer, arranger, and producer. He's produced music for all the great country stars, including Glen Campbell, The Fifth Dimension, Willie Nelson…the list goes on.

When he was 7 years old, his parents sent him to a piano teacher for $10 an hour. She had a special knowledge in chord creation, layering, and some pretty sophisticated stuff.

At $10 an hour. Think about how many people his music impacted because he had a coach when he was 7 years old.

Now you may not think of a piano teacher as a coach, but I do. What else is she? She taught him, held him accountable, and kept him improving. She was a coach.

You

If you want to make exponential improvement in your outcomes, you must have somebody around who can advise you on inputs. Maybe this coach is your manager. Maybe it's a good friend that you find to coach each other.

The bottom line is you need another set of eyes on some of your actions to make sure they are the right actions.

A Small Start

One way to start small on this is to join a **coaching group** of other like-minded professionals who want to expand their reach. These do not have to be people in your industry. In fact, I would suggest some of them **not** be.

You will spend $200 to $1,000 / month for this group. Most of these groups you can join without any kind of a long-term agreement. I suggest small groups (4-8 people) are best. It's best if there is a moderator or a leader to keep people on track.

Make sure there's an **accountability** element of these groups as well. It's always better if you have to report to someone any behavior you commit to.

Your goal in hiring a coach or getting into a group is to **expand what's possible for you.** If you're in a small group, and someone is using a lead generation strategy that you'd never thought of, steal it and use it.

"But Bill, that's a lot of money. That's like a car payment per month." Yes, it is.

And you have to decide if you're worth it. Maybe you're not. Maybe you're happy with your 75k a year, and you don't want to get to $500k / year.

In that case, don't hire a coach. You'll get there eventually, but it might take you 20 years.

One of my favorite clients that I coach from Australia told me that the reason he spends $50,000 a year on coaches is because he wants to get to $5 million in 2 years - not in 22 years. And he's done it.

He does not see coaching as an expense…but as a trade-off. He gives a coach $20k/year, and the coach gives him $200k in income. I know this is foreign to most of you. It was to me until I started to invest in coaching – then I saw how much value I could get out of it.

Don't invest your last dollar in a coach, but get started.

A Good Coach

Just because a coach has accreditation from some certificate factory does not make them a great coach. You can recognize a great coach because they do these things:

1. Spend **a lot** of time upfront understanding who you are, what your background is, and where you're going. They do not jump into tactics. If you hire a coach that rushes to "to-do's", run away quickly.
2. Creates a **Master Plan**. Maybe it's 90 days at a time, but a coach worth his/her weight comes with a plan once they understand #1. I've always felt like counseling ends up being worthless because there's never any plan. It's just 1 hour at a time - $200 at a time. It's ridiculous. A good coach will not do that to you.
3. **The relationship is ongoing.** You do not get coached once for one hour and expect to get anything out of it. You are too complicated to change in one hour. I always suggest 90 days as a starting point, but then continue from there. Never sign up for a one-year coaching program. You need to feel each other out. The coach needs to make sure you're someone who is coachable, and you need to figure out if the coach is worth paying for. **90 Days.** Not 30. Not 365. **90.**

4. **Understands your comfort zone** - and is willing to talk about it. When I first started coaching CEOs, leaders, and salespeople, I would always give them things that were far outside their comfort zone. The mistake I made was not understanding where that zone was. Once I was able to incorporate that in my work, I would give them things that stretched their comfort zone but did not put them into the Panic Zone. Nobody learns in the Panic Zone :)

CHAPTER 10
CREATE A MINI BOOK

You raise your position in the marketplace when you document your perspective on the problems your audience has - and share that with them.

The first version of this book was a mini-book. A mini-book is typically 10 - 40 pages. The idea is to you write up what you know about a situation or an industry – and offer to give or sell at a low price. You can get books published for $4 each from Amazon. Or, it can be a PDF like this one where there is no printing cost. (I would start there).

You will likely need to write it yourself. Get it designed properly, and hire someone on fiverr.com to create a cover for you (less than $100).

There are two hidden benefits to this. 1) You become a published author. It's not going to win a Pulitzer Prize for writing, but that's not what you're looking for. **You want to position yourself** in the marketplace from a place of expertise and experience. And it does that.

And 2) You get good at putting your thoughts into writing. Be concise. Good writers are good communicators - and that skill will serve you for a lifetime.

Yes, you might need to run it past a college English student to pick it apart and correct things that don't flow. Put their name on it as editor…they'll likely do it for their resume.

What Would You Write About?

For this book, I went back and looked at all of my training over the last 6 months. And came up with a list of the 12 most underused **bold moves** that you can deploy to grow your business. You could do the same thing in your business.

For You

You could take the most common questions that customers have for you and create a document called "10 Common Questions" – and send that out prior to a meeting or put it on your website. Or, shoot a LinkedIn video each week covering one of the 10 and offer the book for those who DM you.

The Ultimate Benefits

Usually, I document the benefits of this strategy upfront, but I decided to do it differently this time. So here are the benefits that I believe you will realize if you would take the time to write a mini book.

1. Establishes Expertise: Writing a book positions you as an expert in your field, enhancing your credibility and authority. You do not need to be a 50-year veteran in a business to have expertise. Maybe you sell heavy equipment, and your expertise is in one specific area of that equipment, like tire size or alloy metal construction. Write on that. The rule always is: Write what you know.

2. Generates Leads: A well-crafted mini-book can be an effective lead generation tool, attracting potential customers interested in your expertise. Create a page on your website that asks for someone's first name and email address, and offer the book for free.

3. Improves Personal Brand Visibility: A published book increases your visibility and helps promote your personal or business brand.

4. Facilitates Networking: Having a book can open doors to speaking engagements, interviews, and other networking opportunities. If you want to get really **Bold**, send this book to a handful of podcasts who are looking for guests like you. Books are a great way into those conversations. Then, take those interviews and put them on your website. See how this works? **Bold. Bold. Bold.**

5. Enhances Marketing Efforts: A book can be used as a powerful marketing tool, offering valuable content to prospects and existing clients. Think about it. You're getting ready to make a presentation to 10 people at your prospect company. And instead of sending them a brochure on your company in advance, you send each of them a copy of your mini-book. Don't you think that will position you differently in the marketplace? **Of course, it will.**

6. Improves Writing Skills: The process of writing a book can enhance your writing abilities and communication skills. When I look at the highest of high achievers (those people who are earning $1 million or more), I always see someone who is an **exquisite communicator.** They understand how to tell stories and how to make the complex simple to understand. A book helps you do that.

7. Provides a Sense of Accomplishment: Completing a book can be a significant personal achievement, boosting your confidence and self-esteem. 95% of the people who read this will never write the book. And since you will, it immediately puts you in the **top 5% of achievers.** This book can work for you long after it's published. And since I care about your self-image, I find this to be a great tool to improve it.

CHAPTER 11

RECORD AN INTRODUCTORY VIDEO

Fear not the camera. It is an asset available to you that you aren't using.

Are you ready for bold? Here we go! I want you to create an **Introductory Video** (pre-first call) that you send to prospects **prior** to jumping on a call or having a face-to-face meeting. This is especially useful if they are unfamiliar with you or your company. **The length of this should be < 3 minutes.**

What's In This Video?

The best way to go about the construction of this is to think, "What would they want to know about me or my company, or, how we will execute this upcoming meeting?"

To get you started, here is a good outline:

1. **Introduction.** Your name – and tell them what to expect: "I'm (name) and in this video" I will share with you a, b and c."
2. **About You** (1 min). "I've been in this industry for x years…" (If you want to share a little about your family, that's fine, but do it quickly. Or, if you have interests outside of work, share that here).
3. **Typical Problems.** "The most common problems I see people struggling with in this industry are a, b and c. Make sure you talk about these **as problems** not as solutions. (It's NOT what people want - it's what people WANT TO SOLVE.)

4. **The Upcoming Call.** "In the meeting that we have scheduled, I thought it would be a good idea to share a bit more about our company, get a sense of some of the dilemmas or circumstances that you're facing as you seek to improve your outcomes, and then I can share with you how we work if we get that far."
5. **More Info.** "If you want to learn more about me or our company before our call, you can go to LinkedIn or (company page.)"

The goal of this video is that when you show up, much of the work has already been done. In a way, they feel like they're talking to a celebrity because they've just watched you on video.

Tweaks

Shoot the video and try it in the next five first meetings. You can even ask them if the video helped them understand things better. If 95% of the people don't watch it, then maybe it's worth deleting. I find that even if people don't watch it, **it's the gesture that counts.**

Where to Put It?

Put it on a Dropbox or Google Drive link. You could put it on YouTube, but you likely don't have a channel yet (that's for the next book :) Plus, YouTube can be confusing - too many distractions.

Another place to put it is your LinkedIn **Feature** section. Yes, you will need to turn on your Creator mode. Then, you can link a prospect directly to that video. I would even suggest you put it in your email signature line. "Want to know how I can help, click here."

CHAPTER 12

DECLARE YOUR 'NEXT STEP' OFFER

People will always follow others who have a plan. No plan, no followers. Be clear and specific about the next steps in your process.

We spend a lot of time in our work becoming crystal clear on what your **Ultimate offer** is and how you proclaim it.

But this **bold** move comes before that. The fact is that you are probably in a multiple-call sales process – because you are selling into a business where there are many decision-makers.

The **Next Step Offer** is a specific explanation of what happens next if they decide to go down the path with you.

Example

Let's say you have a first call – and the next call, you recommend there be more of them involved.

You would say, "Here's what I think we should do next– I'm wondering if it would be helpful to have a couple of your people and a couple of my people in the next call. We would send out an agenda beforehand where people can share their perspectives on what they want to address in that meeting. Then, on the call, I would ask each person to share those suggestions. Following that meeting, I would send notes and recommendations based on what we talked about. How does that sound?"

What you're doing here is laying out, **specifically**, what the next step looks like. It's the **offer** to go to the next step. Do this at every junction in the sales process. **Watch what happens to their desire to continue.**

The Rule

Remember, if you've listened to my podcast, you've heard me say that you are the **guide** on their path. YOU are the one that helps them decide whether it's worth engaging or going further.

Anything you can do to keep them on track will be helpful. It's easier for someone to say, "Yes" to something they're crystal clear about.

Very few salespeople do this. You want them to feel like they're in good hands with you as the guide. The clearer you can be about next steps, the better hands they feel they are in.

ADDITIONAL TRAINING

The reason I wrote this document is **I want you to be even more successful than you are right now.**

I realize that you are already good at what you do. Got that.

But I also find that most of us want **more - more money, more joy, more free time - the "more" list is endless**.

And to get **more,** we must **leverage** our capabilities and assets. I trust this book has helped you expand your thinking about what's possible in your business – and given you things you can deploy immediately.

I hope you've enjoyed these sales secrets to the **bold moves** you can make to ramp up your results.

Special Note to VPs/CEOS

The fact is you are in a unique position, as a leader of a team or a company, to bring new thinking into your culture. I know I've given you a lot here and the question always is, "How do I implement or deploy these among my team members?"

Step 1: First off, I would purchase the book (and the audio version) for every member of your team. Yes, it sounds like I'm schlepping books, but I'm really not. Every one of these books, at the price you'll pay for it, could represent hundreds of thousands of dollars of increased revenue for your company.

I know every author says that, but I've seen these things work to improve results for companies just like yours.

Step 2: Once you have this book in everyone's hands, have a sales meeting each month devoted to **one** of these 12 moves. Don't try to handle them all at once. You'll overwhelm your team. But find a way to address one per month. I think you'll be ecstatic about the inspiration that this gives your people.

Step 3: If you believe these **bold moves** would help your sales team, I'm happy to chat about how we can bring these moves into your organization. If you want to schedule a call with me to see what that might look like, go here: www.scheduleacallwithcaskey.com

I typically coach people at three levels:

- <u>The CEO Level</u>
    - How to build a high-quality sales team
    - How to create a sales process that is replicable and predictable

- - How to use the company assets better for customer acquisition.
- The VP Sales/Sales Leader Level
  - How to both instruct and inspire your sales team
  - How to build confidence in their ability to communicate the value to customers
  - How to become a 'world class sales leader' and serve as an example for your team.
- The Sales Professional Level
  - How to change your mindset thereby allowing you to perform at higher levels.
  - How to help deploy a better sales and lead generation strategy
  - How to be mechanically proficient in the areas of persuasion

So, if you'd like to speak about that, refer to the link above and we can jump on a call and talk about what that might look like.

I would like to invite you to participate in our **Million Dollar Seller Challenge** that we do each month in 2024-25. The tuition for this program is $97.

It will take you through a five-day, one-hour per-day overview of how you can generate more clients and more income.

This is not a course or a series of webinars, but a live training. Each day comes with a worksheet that you can use to learn my philosophy and execute in your market.

This is primarily for sales professionals, CEOs, presidents, and anyone who has the responsibility to acquire more customers.

If you'd like to learn more about it, go to **www.milliondollarsellerchallenge.com.** There's a video there that walks you through how it works.

www.ingramcontent.com/pod-product-compliance
Lightning Source LLC
Chambersburg PA
CBHW071953210526
45479CB00003B/916